THE WI BOOK OF FISH AND SEAFOOD

Over 100 recipes tried and tested by the Women's Institutes

MARY NORWAK

EBURY
PRESS

ACKNOWLEDGEMENTS

Illustrated by Vanessa Luff
Edited by Suzanne Luchford
Designed by Julia Golding
Cover photography by James Jackson

Published by Ebury Press
Division of The National Magazine Company Limited
Colquhoun House
27-37 Broadwick Street,
London W1V 1FR

ISBN 0 85223 533 X

First published 1987

© Copyright 1987 WI Books Ltd

Typeset by Central Southern Typesetters, Eastbourne

Reproduced, printed and bound in Great Britain by
Hazell, Watson & Viney Ltd,
Member of the BPCC Group, Aylesbury, Bucks

CONTENTS

INTRODUCTION

Fish is an important source of food. It is nourishing and very quick to prepare. In these health-conscious days, it is important to remember that fish is an excellent source of protein, vitamins and minerals, and that fish oil is polyunsaturated, which helps to lower the body's cholesterol level. Calorific value varies, with 100 g (4 oz) of herring having 190 calories compared to 90 calories in the same amount of sole, but this compares to 350 calories for the same quantity of lamb chop.

There are so many different varieties of fish that menus can be endlessly changed, and a couple of fish meals a week can scarcely be a hardship. Even those who prefer meat will not scorn a fish cocktail or pâté to start a meal, while flans and sandwiches may incorporate fish in a way which appeals to the young eater.

There is a fishmonger in most towns, while villages are often served by a travelling van. Supermarkets now often have a fresh fish department or a special chilled cabinet. However, we need never be deprived of fish in even the most remote areas, for there is now a wide variety of frozen fish available, as well as that traditional favourite – smoked fish. There is also canned fish which is nutritious and tasty and can be turned into some splendid meals.

In this book you will find more than a hundred recipes for fish and their accompanying sauces, about enough for two meals a week to last a whole year. It is hoped that you will want to cook some of them even more often because they will quickly become family favourites.

Choosing and using fish

Frozen and canned fish will have been prepared to exacting standards, so there is no problem in choosing the required quality. Fresh fish, however, needs to be chosen with care and there are one or two easy points to remember.

White fish fillets should be a white translucent colour and a neat shape.

Whole fish should have clear bright eyes, shiny colourful skin, firm flesh and a fresh sea smell.

Smoked fish should have a fresh smoky smell, and the fillets should be neat and firm.

Shellfish should be undamaged in shells and closed tightly without cracks. Ready-cooked shellfish should be moist with a fresh look and smell.

Preparation and storage

A good fishmonger will clean, bone and fillet fish if required, and will also skin fillets or whole fish if necessary. He has the expertise and the sharp knife to do the job, and will always be happy to co-operate with special preparation if you have an unusual dish in mind (but don't expect too much attention on a busy weekend morning).

Fresh fish should be used as soon as possible, but may be stored in the refrigerator overnight if washed, patted dry and covered.

Frozen fish should be stored at −18°C (0°F) or colder, as indicated on the packet. Usually frozen fish may be cooked immediately, but if it is to be defrosted, this is best done overnight in the refrigerator. It should not be thawed in water as it will quickly lose texture, flavour and nutritional value. Fish from the fishmonger should not be frozen, but fish straight from the sea or river may be frozen at home.

Types of fish

One of the advantages of choosing fish is that many species are interchangeable. Whole fish may be bought, as well as fillets and steaks. Fish are basically divided into white and oily varieties. Some white and oily fish are also sold smoked or salted. Shellfish is now often known as 'seafood' and for culinary purposes may be recognised as being of the crustacea or mollusc type.

White fish. There are two types of white fish, divided into flat and round. Large round species such as cod and coley may be sold whole or prepared as fillets, steaks or cutlets. The smaller round fish such as whiting and haddock may be whole or filleted. All these round fish are interchangeable in recipes, varying slightly in flavour and texture.

Large flat fish like turbot and halibut are very special, and may be whole or in fillets and steaks, trimmed as required. The smaller flat fish include plaice, Dover sole and lemon sole, sold whole or in fillets.

Unusual flat fish include the monkfish (anglerfish) of which only the tail is eaten, tasting rather like scampi and with a similar texture. Skate is another delicious flat fish, of which the 'wings' are generally sold, ready-skinned. Odd round fish include the conger eel, the rather ugly John Dory, grey mullet, and red mullet which has a slightly 'gamey' flavour and is usually eaten uncleaned. If you do not recognise these fish, the fishmonger will be glad to tell you about them and to prepare them for cooking.

Oily fish. These tend to be smaller than other species, and are a particularly rich source of vitamins A and D. Herring, mackerel and sprat are the most commonly found, and they are sold whole, though often boned or filleted for cooking. Salmon also comes into this group.

Smoked and salted fish. Some white fish may be smoked, particularly cod, haddock and whiting, although smoked halibut is sometimes found, and is a great delicacy. Smoked salmon and trout are often regarded as special occasion fish. The herring is one of the most adaptable fish, being salted or marinated, but also being smoked and appearing as the kipper or bloater. The small sprat may also be smoked and served on special occasions. In recent times, mackerel has become a very popular smoked fish, and may be prepared in two ways. Cold smoked mackerel and kippers have a smoky flavour but are still raw and must be cooked. Hot smoked mackerel is prepared at a higher temperature so that the flesh cooks and the fish are ready to eat.

Seafood (shellfish). Scallops, mussels, oysters, cockles, whelks and winkles are distinguished by their very hard shells. Oysters are generally eaten raw and can be opened by the fishmonger (if you have to do the job yourself, the shell is opened by inserting a knife through the hinge of the shell). Scallops and the smaller Queens may be sold in the shell or loose, and the deep shell is used for serving the cooked dish. Mussels need to be scrubbed and the 'beards' removed before steaming open, but the fishmonger may have a supply of freshly cooked ones. The same applies to cockles and whelks. Winkles are sold ready cooked but still in the shell.

Lobsters, crabs, prawns, shrimps and scampi (Dublin bay prawns) are recognised by their bright pinky-red shells when cooked. Prawns, shrimps and scampi may be sold in the shell or ready peeled. Crabs and lobsters are generally sold boiled but not prepared, but some fishmongers sell dressed crabs.

Canned fish. A wide variety of fish is canned in oil, brine or tomato sauce. Popular varieties include sardines, salmon, tuna, pilchard and mackerel, but it is also possible to find kipper fillets, herring roes, prawns, shrimps, clams and oysters. All of these are useful for the store cupboard.

Fish cookery

Whichever method is chosen, fish should never be overcooked. The flesh should be just set so that it remains moist and full of flavour.

Boiling. This is only recommended for large pieces of fish. The fish should be rubbed with lemon juice to keep it firm and white, then cooked in hot salted water or Court Bouillon (see page 91). Cook the fish in a large shallow pan or fish kettle, if possible in a piece of muslin or foil so that the fish can be lifted out without breaking. Bring the liquid to the boil and then simmer very gently until the fish is just cooked and ready to flake away from the bone. Timing depends on the thickness and shape of the fish, but usually 10–15 minutes per 450 g (1 lb) is enough. Drain the fish well before serving.

Poaching. Small pieces of fish or small whole fish may be cooked in this way. If poaching fillets, fold or roll them before cooking. Use milk, fish stock, or a mixture of milk and water in a saucepan or frying pan, and half-cover the fish with liquid. Simmer gently for 10 minutes per 450 g (1 lb). Drain and use the cooking liquid for an accompanying sauce.

Steaming. Thin pieces and fillets are best suited to steaming. Place the fish directly in a steamer over a pan of boiling water, and allow 15 minutes to 450 g (1 lb) plus 15 minutes for large fish (fillets will take 20 minutes). Small fillets or cutlets may be cooked on a greased deep plate with 1 tablespoon milk and seasoning over a pan of boiling water, covered with a second plate or lid – this method is particularly attractive for invalid dishes.

Shallow frying. Allow just enough fat or oil to prevent the fish sticking, and use a shallow pan. When the fat or oil is just smoking, cook the fish quickly on both sides for a few minutes until golden brown, and finish cooking gently until the flesh loosens from the bone. For shallow frying, the fish may be lightly coated with flour; or with flour, milk and flour again; or with flour, beaten egg and breadcrumbs. The fish should not be prepared until just before frying.

Butter frying. A simple and delicious frying method suitable for fillets of flat fish and for small whole fish, if not more than 1 cm (½ in) thick. Dip the fish in seasoned flour, shake off the surplus, and then cook on both sides in hot butter. For 4 fillets, allow 50 g (2 oz) butter and cook for about 5 minutes each side. Place the fish on a serving dish without draining. Add a knob of extra butter to the pan and when hot and frothy, add the juice of half a lemon. Pour over the fish and sprinkle with chopped fresh parsley.

Deep frying. The fish should be coated with egg and breadcrumbs (see Shallow frying) or coated with Batter (see page 91). Use a deep pan and wire basket and enough fat to come three-quarters of the way up the pan. Use oil, clarified beef fat or lard, and make sure that the fat is pure and free from moisture. Heat the fat to 180–190°C (350–375°F). Put the fish into the wire basket and place in the hot fat. When the fish is golden, lift out the basket from the fat and drain the fried fish well on absorbent kitchen paper.

Stir frying. A new and popular way of cooking fish quickly which uses only a small amount of oil. Use a wok or sauté pan and a tablespoon of oil (peanut oil is particularly good). Heat the pan and add finely chopped seasonal vegetables and small cubes of fish. Toss quickly over the heat and serve as soon as the fish has become opaque.

Grilling. Fillets and cutlets may be grilled after being seasoned and sprinkled with lemon juice and brushed well with melted butter or oil. The time taken under a medium grill is from 3–7 minutes on each side, depending on the thickness of the fish. Since fish tends to stick to the wire grill rack, it is best to line the grill pan with foil and to place the fish directly on this (which also makes the pan easier to clean). Whole fish should be scaled first and scored two or three times with a sharp knife on each side. For *barbecuing*, brush the fish well with oil, lemon juice and herbs, and baste it occasionally during cooking, so that the fish remains moist.

Baking. An excellent method for cooking whole fish in a greased dish, well-seasoned with salt, pepper and lemon juice. A little milk or water should be poured round the fish, which should be covered with a piece of greased paper. Allow 10–15 minutes per 450 g (1 lb) in a moderate oven, 180°C (350°F) mark 4, depending on the thickness of the fish and whether it is stuffed. As an alternative, the fish may be simply brushed with melted butter and sprinkled with breadcrumbs before baking; this is particularly suitable for cutlets. *Foil-baking* is excellent for cutlets, tail-ends of fish, or small whole fish, such as salmon or trout. Wrap the fish in well-buttered foil with plenty of seasoning, lemon juice and fresh herbs. Place the foil packet on a baking sheet and allow 20 minutes per 450 g (1 lb) in a moderate oven, 180°C (350°F) mark 4. The fish is exceptionally moist and full of juices when cooked by this method.

Microwaving. Fish cooked in the microwave is full of flavour with an excellent texture and appearance. Add a little lemon juice and seasoning, slit the fish skin in two or three places to prevent bursting, and cover the fish with microwave-proof film. For timing, consult the manufacturer's booklet.

Covering

Cook, uncovered, unless otherwise stated. The use of cling film should be avoided in microwave cooking, use microwave-proof film. When a recipe requires you to cover the container, you should either cover with a lid or a plate, leaving a gap to let steam escape.

Measurements

All recipes are given in metric and imperial quantities. When following the recipes, use either metric measurements or imperial: do not mix the two.

Eggs are size 2 or 3 unless stated otherwise.

All spoon measurements are level unless stated otherwise.

American equivalents

	Metric	Imperial	American
Margarine	225 g	8 oz	1 cup
Cheese (grated)	100 g	4 oz	1 cup
Flour	100 g	4 oz	1 cup
Rice	225 g	8 oz	1 cup

An American pint is 16 fl oz compared with the imperial pint of 20 fl oz. A standard American cup measure is considered to hold 8 fl oz.

WHITE FISH

An interesting collection of recipes for everyday
use and special occasions, from Cornish Cod to
Summer Fish Terrine.

SAVOURY BREAD AND BUTTER PUDDING

Serves 4

8 medium-thick bread slices
75 g (3 oz) butter
150 g (5 oz) Cheddar cheese, grated
350 g (12 oz) white fish
275 ml (½ pint) milk
150 ml (¼ pint) single cream
2 eggs
salt and pepper
few drops of Tabasco sauce

Heat the oven to 180°C (350°F) mark 4. Remove the crusts from the bread. Spread the bread generously with butter and sprinkle with grated cheese. Cut each slice in half. Remove the bones and skin from the fish and cut the flesh into small pieces. Arrange a layer of bread in an oven-proof dish. Add half the fish and spread it over the bread, then add another layer of bread. Top with the remaining fish and the remaining bread with the cheese uppermost.

Beat together the milk, cream and eggs and season well with salt, pepper and Tabasco sauce. Pour over the bread. Leave to stand for 1 hour. Bake for 45 minutes.

Serve hot with vegetables or a salad.

FISH CRUMBLE

Serves 4

450 g (1 lb) white fish, cooked
75 g (3 oz) butter
1 small onion, finely chopped
4 tomatoes, skinned
1 garlic clove, crushed
1 tbsp fresh parsley, chopped
1 tbsp lemon juice
150 ml (¼ pint) water
1 tbsp cornflour
salt and pepper
75 g (3 oz) plain flour

Heat the oven to 220°C (425°F) mark 7. Flake the fish into a bowl. Melt 25 g (1 oz) of the butter and cook the onion until soft and golden. Discard the seeds from the tomatoes and chop the flesh roughly. Add the tomatoes to the onion with the garlic, parsley, lemon juice and water and simmer for 5 minutes. Mix the cornflour with a little water and stir into the sauce. Simmer for 3 minutes and season well with salt and pepper. Stir in the flaked fish and put the mixture into a greased oven-proof dish. Rub the remaining butter into the flour and sprinkle over the fish. Bake for 20 minutes and serve hot.

A few button mushrooms may be added to the sauce, or some peeled prawns, chopped green pepper or cooked peas, or a mixture of these added ingredients.

FRENCH FISH CASSEROLE

Serves 4

450 g (1 lb) leeks
50 g (2 oz) butter
1 green pepper, sliced
225 g (8 oz) tomatoes, quartered
salt and pepper
675 g (1½ lb) white fish fillets
1 tbsp lemon juice
1 tbsp fresh parsley, chopped

Heat the oven to 180°C (350°F) mark 4. Clean the leeks well and chop into 2.5 cm (1 in) chunks. Melt 40 g (1½ oz) of the butter and cook the leeks and pepper until soft and golden. Stir in the tomatoes and season well with salt and pepper. Spoon into a greased oven-proof dish. Cut the fish into 4 portions and place on top of the mixture. Sprinkle with lemon juice and parsley and dot with the remaining butter. Cover and bake for 25 minutes. Remove the cover and continue baking for 5 minutes.

Serve at once with boiled potatoes.

FRUITED FISH CURRY

Serves 4

675 g (1½ lb) white fish
1 medium onion, finely chopped
40 g (1½ oz) butter
1 tbsp curry paste
2 tbsp fruit chutney
1 tbsp sultanas
1 eating apple
40 g (1½ oz) plain flour
275 g (10 oz) long grain rice
1 egg, hard-boiled
100 g (4 oz) prawns, shelled
   (optional)

Skin the fish, remove the bones and cut into serving portions. Cover with water and simmer for 10 minutes. Drain the fish and keep warm, and reserve the cooking liquid for stock. Fry the onion in the butter until soft and golden. Stir in the curry paste and cook for 1 minute. Add the chutney and sultanas. Do not peel the apple, but core and cut the flesh into dice. Stir into the pan and add the flour. Cook until the flour is golden, mixing all the time.

Measure the fish stock and make up to 425 ml (¾ pint) of liquid with water, add to the pan. Bring to the boil and then simmer and stir until the sauce is smooth. Put the fish pieces into the pan and reheat. While the sauce is cooking, boil the rice in salted water for 12–15 minutes and drain well. Arrange the rice in a border on a hot dish and spoon in the fish. Garnish with chopped egg, and prawns if liked.

BAKED FISH CHARLOTTE

Serves 4

350 g (12 oz) white fish fillets
275 ml (½ pint) white sauce
  (see page 87)
1 garlic clove, crushed
225 g (8 oz) tomatoes
75 g (3 oz) fresh white or brown
  breadcrumbs
salt and pepper
50 g (2 oz) butter

Heat the oven to 220°C (425°F) mark 7. Poach the fish, cool and remove the skin and any bones. Flake the fish and mix with the white sauce and garlic. Skin the tomatoes and slice them thickly. Put half the fish mixture into a greased pie dish and top with a layer of tomatoes and breadcrumbs, seasoning the layers with salt and pepper. Repeat the layers and dot with flakes of butter. Bake for 20 minutes.

Serve hot with a vegetable or salad.

FISH FLORENTINE

Serves 4

675 g (1½ lb) white fish fillets
450 g (1 lb) frozen leaf spinach or
  675 g (1½ lb) fresh spinach
salt and pepper
275 ml (½ pint) cheese sauce
  (see variation, page 87)
pinch of cayenne pepper
25 g (1 oz) Parmesan cheese, grated

Skin the fish fillets and poach them until just tender. Drain and keep warm. Cook the frozen spinach according to packet instructions, or steam the fresh spinach until cooked. Drain very well and press out as much liquid as possible. Season the spinach and arrange in a buttered oven-proof dish. Place the fish portions on top. Season the cheese sauce well with salt, pepper and cayenne pepper. Spoon over the cheese sauce and sprinkle on the Parmesan cheese. Place under a hot grill until the surface is brown and bubbling. Serve at once.

WINTER FISH CASSEROLE

Serves 4

675 g (1½ lb) white fish
50 g (2 oz) streaky bacon
40 g (1½ oz) butter
225 g (8 oz) potatoes
225 g (8 oz) carrots
100 g (4 oz) turnips
1 medium onion
1 bay leaf
salt and pepper
275 ml (½ pint) dry cider
25 g (1 oz) plain flour
150 ml (¼ pint) milk

Heat the oven to 190°C (375°F) mark 5. Skin the fish and cut into cubes. Chop the bacon roughly. Melt the butter and stir in the fish and bacon. Cook over a low heat until the fish is golden brown on all sides. Peel the vegetables. Cut the potatoes into cubes and dice the carrots and turnips. Slice the onion thinly. Add the vegetables to the pan and stir well. Put the mixture into a casserole and place the bay leaf on top. Season well with salt and pepper. Pour in the cider and cover and bake for 30 minutes.

Mix the flour with a little of the milk to make a smooth paste and then add the remaining milk. Stir into the casserole, return to oven and continue baking for 10 minutes.

Serve hot with potatoes or rice if liked, or with plenty of crusty bread.

SUMMER FISH SALAD

Serves 4

450 g (1 lb) white fish fillets
2 hard-boiled eggs, chopped
4 anchovy fillets, finely chopped
2 gherkins, finely chopped
2 tsp capers
2 tbsp olive oil
2 tsp lemon juice
1 tbsp chopped fresh chives
pepper
150 ml (¼ pint) mayonnaise

Poach the fish until just tender. Cool and break into flakes. Mix with the eggs, anchovies, gherkins and capers. Stir together the oil and lemon juice with the chives and plenty of pepper. Pour over the fish and toss lightly. Press lightly into a shallow serving dish and spoon over the mayonnaise. Chill and serve with a green salad and thin brown bread and butter.

SPANISH FISH SALAD

Serves 4

450 g (1 lb) white fish or smoked
  haddock fillets
225 g (8 oz) long-grain rice
salt and pepper
4 tbsp olive oil
1½ tbsp white wine vinegar
1 garlic clove, crushed
½ tsp French mustard
2 large tomatoes, skinned
4 spring onions
7.5 cm (3 in) cucumber, peeled
1 green pepper, finely chopped
1 red pepper, finely chopped

Poach the fish until tender. Cool and break
into flakes. Meanwhile boil the rice in salted
water until tender. Drain well, rinse in cold
water, drain and leave in a bowl until cool
but not cold.

Mix together the oil, vinegar, garlic,
mustard, salt and pepper. Discard the pips
from tomatoes and chop the flesh roughly.
Chop the spring onions finely. Discard the
seeds from cucumber and dice the flesh
finely. Mix the fish, peppers, tomatoes,
onions and cucumber into the rice and add
the dressing. Toss lightly so that the fish
does not break into very small pieces. Chill
before serving. Peeled prawns or shrimps
may be added before serving.

FISH CREAMS

Serves 4–6

225 g (8 oz) white fish
25 g (1 oz) melted butter
225 g (8 oz) peeled prawns
150 ml (¼ pint) white sauce (see
  page 87)
1 egg white
salt and pepper
pinch of ground mace
pinch of cayenne pepper
150 ml (¼ pint) double cream

Heat the oven to 180°C (350°F) mark 4.
Poach the fish until just tender. Drain well
and remove the skin. Put into a food
processor or liquidiser with the butter and
150 g (6 oz) of the prawns. Blend until
smooth. Add the white sauce and egg white
and blend until very smooth. Season well
with salt and pepper, mace and cayenne
pepper.

Whip the cream to soft peaks and fold
into the fish mixture. Place the remaining
prawns in four to six individual oven-proof
dishes. Top with the fish mixture. Place the
dishes in a baking tin with hot water to
come halfway up the dishes. Cover with
greased greaseproof paper. Bake for 30
minutes.

Serve with Hollandaise or Tomato Sauce
(see page 86).

GRANNY'S FISH SUPPER

Serves 4

675 g (1½ lb) white fish fillets
4 medium onions, thinly sliced
oil or fat for frying
4 medium potatoes, boiled
salt and pepper
25 g (1 oz) Cheddar cheese, grated
1 tbsp fresh parsley, chopped

The fish may be cod, haddock, coley or any other white fish. Poach the fish, cool slightly and remove the skin and any bones. Break into flakes. Fry the onions in a little hot oil or fat until soft and golden, and drain well. Slice the potatoes thinly. Grease an oven-proof dish and put in a layer of potatoes, then onion and fish, seasoning lightly. Continue in layers, finishing with a layer of potatoes. Sprinkle with cheese. Either bake at 180°C (350°F) mark 4 for 25 minutes *or* put under a hot grill to brown if the ingredients are freshly cooked and still hot. Sprinkle with parsley and serve.

This is a useful supper dish as it may be assembled early in the day and refrigerated until needed.

FISH CORKS

Serves 4

225 g (8 oz) white fish, cooked
275 ml (½ pint) parsley sauce
  (see page 85)
25 g (1 oz) fresh white or brown
  breadcrumbs
2 eggs
salt and pepper
25 g (1 oz) plain flour
6 tbsp dry breadcrumbs
oil for frying

Flake the fish into a bowl. Cook the parsley sauce until it is thick enough to hold a peak. Mix the fish, sauce and fresh breadcrumbs together. Beat the eggs and add just enough to bind the mixture. Season well with salt and pepper. Leave until completely cold and then form into a long sausage on a floured board, making the cylinder about 2.5 cm (1 in) thick. Cut into 5 cm (2 in) lengths. Dip in the flour, then beaten egg and finally the dry breadcrumbs. Fry in hot oil until golden brown and serve at once.

These are a delicious home-made alternative to the fish finger. Some smoked fish may be included if liked.

PAELLA

Serves 8–10

675 g (1½ lb) long grain rice
1 chicken, cut into 8–10 pieces
450 g (1 lb) lean pork, diced
3 tbsp oil
1 large onion, finely chopped
3 ripe tomatoes
225 g (8 oz) peas
3 red peppers, chopped
350 g (12 oz) white fish (cod,
  haddock, hake)
16 mussels in shells
225 g (8 oz) prawns in shells
1 tsp salt
½ tsp pepper
pinch of saffron

A large deep frying pan is best for the preparation of this dish. Ingredients may be varied – runner beans are often substituted for peas. Pieces of eel, crab or lobster may be added to the fish.

Rinse the rice in cold water and drain well. Put the chicken pieces and pork into a pan with the hot oil and cook until brown, add the onion and over a low heat, stirring well, cook until the onion is soft and golden. Peel and deseed the tomatoes. Chop the flesh roughly and add to the pan. Stir and cook for 3 minutes and then add the rice. Cook and stir over a low heat for 10 minutes. Add the peas and peppers; cook for 5 minutes. Add the pieces of fish, and mussels in their shells. Peel half the prawns and add to the pan. Season with salt and pepper and simmer for 10 minutes.

Add the saffron and stir in 1.8 litres (3 pints) boiling water. Bring to the boil and then simmer until the rice is cooked and all the water has been absorbed, stirring occasionally. Stir in the prawns in their shells. To give the paella a rich golden colour, put the pan into a low oven, 170°C (325°F) mark 3, for 5 minutes. Remove from the oven and leave to stand for 2 minutes so that the mixture blends and settles before serving.

WHITE FISH SUPPER BAKE

Serves 4

450 g (1 lb) white fish
1 medium onion, chopped
2 eggs, beaten
275 ml (½ pint) milk
75 g (3 oz) butter, softened
75 g (3 oz) fresh white or brown
  breadcrumbs
1 tbsp lemon juice
salt and pepper
50 g (2 oz) Cheddar cheese, grated

Heat the oven to 190°C (375°F) mark 5. Poach the fish until just tender and cool. Flake the fish into a bowl. Add the onion, beaten eggs, milk, butter, breadcrumbs, lemon juice and salt and pepper. Put into a greased oven-proof dish and sprinkle with cheese. Bake for 40 minutes.

Serve hot with a mushroom or tomato sauce and crusty bread.

HUNGARIAN FISH CASSEROLE

Serves 4–6

6 cod cutlets
40 g (1½ oz) butter
2 medium onions, thinly sliced
1 tbsp paprika
25 g (1 oz) plain flour
275 ml (½ pint) milk
225 g (8 oz) canned tomatoes
salt and pepper
150 ml (¼ pint) soured cream

Heat the oven to 180°C (350°F) mark 4. Place the fish in an oven-proof dish in a single layer. Melt the butter in a pan and add the onions. Cook over a low heat for 5 minutes, stirring well, until the onions are soft and golden. Stir in the paprika and cook for 1 minute. Stir in the flour and cook for 1 minute. Gradually add the milk and the tomatoes with their juice. Break up the tomatoes with a fork. Bring to the boil and then simmer for 20 minutes.

Season well with salt and pepper and pour over the fish. Cover and cook for 45 minutes. Remove the lid and spoon the soured cream on top of the fish. Serve at once with rice or noodles and a green salad.

SUMMER FISH TERRINE

Serves 6–8

100 g (4 oz) courgettes
100 g (4 oz) French beans
100 g (4 oz) carrots
900 g (2 lb) cod or haddock
50 g (2 oz) fresh white breadcrumbs
4 tbsp double cream
2 tbsp French mustard
2 tbsp lemon juice
2 tbsp dry vermouth
salt and pepper

Heat the oven to 180°C (350°F) mark 4. Wipe the courgettes but to not peel them. Trim the ends and cut into sticks the same size as the beans. Peel the carrots and cut to the same size as the beans. Blanch each vegetable in boiling water for 5 minutes. Drain and dry well and keep to one side. Skin the fish and mince (or use a food processor) with the breadcrumbs, cream, mustard, lemon juice and vermouth. Season well with salt and pepper.

Butter a 1-litre (2-pint) terrine or loaf tin. Spread one-quarter of the fish mixture over the base. Arrange the beans lengthwise on top. Spread on a second quarter of fish mixture and top with the carrots arranged lengthwise. Put on the third quarter of the fish mixture, the courgettes lengthwise and the final layer of fish. Cover with a buttered piece of greaseproof paper and foil or a lid. Place the container in a roasting tin containing 2.5 cm (1 in) water. Bake for 50 minutes. Leave to stand for 30 minutes. Drain off any liquid and unmould on a serving dish. Slice carefully and serve warm or cold as a first course, or with salad.

COD IN TOMATO SAUCE

Serves 4

4 cod steaks
1 large onion, finely chopped
100 g (4 oz) streaky bacon rashers,
  chopped
1/2 green pepper
1 tbsp oil
450 g (1 lb) canned tomatoes
1/2 tsp fresh mixed herbs
salt and pepper

Grill or fry the cod steaks until golden on both sides. While the fish is cooking, fry the onion, bacon and pepper in oil for 5 minutes over a low heat, stirring well. Add the tomatoes and their juice with the herbs, salt and pepper. Bring to the boil and simmer for 10 minutes. Place the cod steaks on a warm serving dish and pour over the sauce. Serve at once with boiled potatoes or crusty bread.

The sauce is very quickly made and may be served with any white fish or with seafood such as scallops or scampi which can be prepared while the sauce is cooking.

PORTUGUESE COD

Serves 4

4 cod steaks
salt and pepper
275 ml (1/2 pint) water
juice of 2 lemons
1 medium onion, chopped
1 garlic clove, crushed
4 tomatoes, peeled and chopped
25 g (1 oz) butter
1 tbsp fresh parsley, chopped
pinch of thyme
100 g (4 oz) button mushrooms

Heat the oven to 180°C (350°F) mark 4. Arrange the cod steaks in a greased oven-proof dish and sprinkle with salt and pepper. Cover with a piece of foil and bake for 10 minutes. While the fish is cooking, put the water, lemon juice, onion, garlic, tomatoes and butter into a pan and simmer together for 10 minutes. Add the parsley, thyme and small whole mushrooms.

Remove the foil from the fish and pour over the sauce. Continue baking for 15 minutes.

Serve with potatoes or rice and a green salad.

CORNISH COD

Serves 4

675 g (1½ lb) cod fillets
salt and pepper
milk
plain flour
75 g (3 oz) butter
24 mussels, cooked
100 g (4 oz) prawns or shrimps,
*   peeled*
2 tsp lemon juice
1 tbsp fresh parsley, chopped
lemon wedges to garnish

Divide the fish into 4 fillets and season with salt and pepper. Dip in the milk and then flour. Melt 50 g (2 oz) of the butter and fry the fish on both sides until golden. Place on a warm serving dish and keep hot. In a clean pan, melt the remaining butter and toss the mussels and prawns or shrimps over a low heat. Add the lemon juice and pour the mixture over the fish. Sprinkle with parsley and serve at once with lemon wedges to garnish.

The mussel and prawn or shrimp garnish may be used for other white fish, including plaice or sole. For a less rich dish, the fish may be grilled if preferred.

FISH PUDDING

Serves 4

450 g (1 lb) cod fillets
1 small onion
575 ml (1 pint) white sauce
*   (see page 87)*
50 g (2 oz) fresh white breadcrumbs
2 eggs
salt and pepper

Skin the fish and cut the flesh into pieces. Mince the fish and onion, or blend together in a food processor. Mix with the white sauce, breadcrumbs and beaten eggs. Season well with salt and pepper. Spoon into a well-greased 750-ml (1½-pint) pudding basin. Cover with greaseproof paper and foil and steam for 1 hour. Turn out and serve with parsley sauce (see page 85). Garnish with a few prawns or some button mushrooms tossed in a little butter.

If preferred, the mixture may be placed in a pie dish and baked at 180°C (350°F) mark 4 for 1 hour, when it will puff up and be golden-brown on the surface.

RUSSIAN FISH PASTRY

Serves 4

225 g (8 oz) shortcrust pastry
  (see page 93)
225 g (8 oz) cod, smoked haddock or
  salmon, cooked
2 large mushrooms, thinly sliced
1 medium onion, finely chopped
100 g (4 oz) long-grain rice, boiled
1 tbsp fresh parsley, chopped
salt and pepper
2 hard-boiled eggs, sliced
egg for glazing

Heat the oven to 200°C (400°F) mark 6. Roll out the pastry into a 25 cm (10 in) square. Flake the fish and mix with the mushrooms, onion, rice, parsley, salt and pepper. Place half the mixture in the centre of the pastry. Place the sliced eggs on top and cover with remaining mixture. Fold over the two sides of the pastry, overlapping them and sealing with a little beaten egg. Seal the ends firmly with beaten egg. Place on a lightly greased baking sheet with the join downwards. Brush well with egg and make two or three diagonal slashes in the top of the pastry. Bake for 25–30 minutes until golden-brown.

Serve hot with Tomato Sauce (see page 86).

FISH CAKES

Serves 4–6

450 g (1 lb) cooked fish, flaked
450 g (1 lb) cooked potatoes
4 tbsp milk
50 g (2 oz) butter, melted
1 egg yolk
1 tbsp fresh parsley, chopped
1 tsp lemon juice
salt and pepper
flour
oil for frying

The fish may be white fish, smoked haddock or kippers, or salmon, or a mixture of smoked fish and white fish may be used. Put the fish into a large bowl. Mash the potatoes with the milk and butter. Add to the fish and mix well and work in the egg yolk, parsley, lemon juice and plenty of salt and pepper. Shape the mixture into 12 round cakes and flatten them slightly. Dust lightly with flour and fry in shallow oil until golden on each side. If preferred, the fishcakes may be dipped in flour, egg and then breadcrumbs before frying.

FISHERMAN'S CHOWDER

Serves 6–8

*900 g (2 lb) mixed smoked and
    white fish
50 g (2 oz) butter
1 large onion, thinly sliced
100 g (4 oz) bacon, chopped
4 celery sticks, chopped
1 red or green pepper, chopped
1 large potato, diced
575 ml (1 pint) water
1 tbsp cornflour
575 ml (1 pint) creamy milk
salt and pepper*

Use a mixture of smoked haddock or cod fillets with some coley, cod, haddock or whiting. Skin the fish and cut into cubes. Melt the butter in a large pan and add the onion, bacon, celery, pepper and potato. Stir over a low heat for 5 minutes. Add the water and simmer for 5 minutes. Add the fish cubes and continue simmering for a further 5 minutes. Blend the cornflour with a little of the milk. Stir in the remaining milk and add to the pan. Season well with salt and pepper and stir over a low heat until the liquid has thickened slightly.

Serve hot with crusty white or wholemeal bread.

GRAPEFRUIT GRILLED FISH

Serves 4

*butter
4 haddock or cod steaks
few drops of Tabasco sauce
salt and pepper
paprika
1 grapefruit*

Line a grill pan with foil and grease the foil lightly with a little butter. Put fish in pan and sprinkle with Tabasco sauce, salt, pepper and paprika. Grill for 4 minutes on each side. Meanwhile peel the grapefruit and cut off all the white pith. Remove the grapefruit segments with a sharp knife so that they are unskinned. Arrange the segments on top of the fish and continue grilling for 4 minutes.

Serve with vegetables or a salad.

HADDOCK WITH GRAPE SAUCE

Serves 4

675 g (1½ lb) haddock fillets
25 g (1 oz) butter
25 g (1 oz) plain flour
3 tbsp double cream
100 g (4 oz) white grapes, peeled
salt and white pepper

Skin the fish and cut into 4 even-sized portions. Poach in water until tender but unbroken, reserve the liquid. Lift carefully on to a serving dish and keep warm. Melt the butter and work in the flour, and stir over a low heat for 1 minute. Add 275 ml (½ pint) of the cooking liquid and stir over a low heat until smooth and creamy. Stir in 2 tablespoons cream and take off the heat. Add peeled and halved grapes, and season to taste. Pour over the fish. Drizzle the remaining cream on top and put under a hot grill to glaze.

BAKED STUFFED HADDOCK

Serves 6

900 g (2 lb) whole haddock
2 tbsp oatmeal
2 tbsp dripping, melted
1 small onion, finely chopped
2 tsp fresh parsley, chopped
2 tsp fresh thyme
salt and pepper
25 g (1 oz) butter, melted
25 g (1 oz) fresh white or brown
    breadcrumbs

Heat the oven to 190°C (375°F) mark 5. Clean the fish and leave whole. Mix together the oatmeal, dripping, onion, herbs and plenty of seasoning. Stuff the fish and close the opening with cocktail sticks. Put the fish into a well-greased oven-proof dish and brush the surface of the fish with a little of the butter. Bake for 30 minutes, basting once or twice. Sprinkle the surface of the fish with the breadcrumbs and sprinkle on the remaining butter. Cover with greaseproof paper and bake at 200°C (400°F) mark 6 for 20 minutes. Remove the cocktail sticks before serving.

MEXICAN FISH SALAD

Serves 4

450 g (1 lb) halibut or haddock
*   fillets*
4 limes
1 crisp lettuce
4 tomatoes, skinned
1 green pepper, finely chopped
4 tbsp olive oil
1 tbsp wine vinegar
2 tbsp fresh parsley, chopped
2 tbsp fresh marjoram, chopped
salt and pepper

Skin the fish and remove any bones. Cut into small cubes and put into a shallow dish. Grate the rind from 1 lime and squeeze out all the juice from all the limes. Sprinkle the rind and juice over the fish, cover and leave in the refrigerator for at least 3 hours. Arrange the lettuce leaves in a serving bowl. Discard the seeds from the tomatoes and chop the flesh roughly. Mix the tomato and pepper pieces and arrange in the bowl. Mix the oil, vinegar, parsley, marjoram, salt and pepper together and sprinkle over the tomatoes. Arrange the fish on top.

The fresh lime juice has the effect of cooking the fish, which retains a beautifully fresh flavour. Bottled lime juice cordial should *not* be used for the dish.

BRITTANY HALIBUT

Serves 4

675 g (1½ lb) halibut fillets
50 g (2 oz) butter
1 medium onion, finely chopped
25 g (1 oz) plain flour
150 ml (¼ pint) dry cider or dry
white wine
2 garlic cloves, crushed
2 tbsp fresh parsley, chopped
2 tbsp lemon juice
salt and pepper
pinch of cayenne pepper
flour
oil for frying

Divide the fish into 4 pieces. Melt the butter and cook the onion over a low heat until soft and golden. Stir in the flour and cook for 1 minute. Stir in the cider or wine, with the garlic and parsley. Simmer for 5 minutes. Add the lemon juice and season well with salt, pepper and cayenne pepper.

While the sauce is cooking, flour the fish lightly and cook in a little hot oil for 3 minutes each side until just golden. Put the fish in a single layer in a shallow oven-proof dish and cover with the sauce. Place under a hot grill for 2–3 minutes until golden and bubbling, and serve at once with boiled potatoes. Cod or haddock may be used instead of halibut.

HALIBUT AND HORSERADISH

Serves 4

675 g (1½ lb) halibut steaks, boned
150 ml (¼ pint) white sauce
(see page 87)
150 ml (¼ pint) single cream
3 egg yolks
1 tbsp horseradish cream
1 tbsp wine vinegar
salt and pepper
1 hard-boiled egg, finely chopped

Heat the oven to 180°C (350°F) mark 4. Place the halibut steaks in a greased oven-proof dish. Add 3 tablespoons of water, cover and bake for 20 minutes. Drain off the liquid and place the fish on a serving dish to keep warm. Warm the white sauce and remove from the heat. Beat in the cream and egg yolks and heat just enough to warm through, but do not boil. Stir in the horseradish cream, vinegar and seasoning. Coat the fish with the sauce and sprinkle with chopped egg.

Serve at once with boiled or sauté potatoes and peas.

NORFOLK FISH PIE

Serves 6

450 g (1 lb) halibut, haddock or cod
225 g (8 oz) lobster or scampi
4 scallops
butter
100 g (4 oz) shrimps, peeled
100 g (4 oz) button mushrooms
4 eggs
275 ml (½ pint) white sauce
    (see page 87)
salt and pepper
450 g (1 lb) mashed potatoes

Heat the oven to 180°C (350°F) mark 4. Poach the white fish and flake the flesh into large pieces. Mix with the lobster or scampi. Remove the corals from the scallops and cut the white part into two circles. Cook for 2 minutes in a little butter and mix the white parts and corals with the white fish. Stir in the shrimps. Wipe the mushrooms but do not peel and cook in the butter for 2 minutes. Stir into the fish. Beat the eggs into the white sauce and add all the fish mixture. Season well and put into a pie dish. Cover with the mashed potatoes and mark lightly with a fork. Bake for 30 minutes.

This is a rich and delicious fish pie, but the ingredients may be varied according to season and budget. Some smoked haddock may be included, mussels may be added and prawns may be used, but the important thing is to get a variety of texture, colour and flavour. The fish may be fresh, canned or frozen, so it is always possible to get an interesting mixture, and while the result is a little expensive, the pie is good enough for a really special meal with guests.

TROUT WITH ALMONDS

Serves 2

2 rainbow trout
25 g (1 oz) plain flour
salt and pepper
100 g (4 oz) butter
50 g (2 oz) flaked almonds
1 tsp lemon juice

Clean and gut the trout but leave the heads and tails intact. Season the flour well with salt and pepper and lightly coat the trout with the flour. Melt half the butter and fry the trout over a low heat for 5 minutes each side. Lift the fish on to a warm serving dish. Add the remaining butter to the pan and toss the almonds over a medium heat until golden. Add lemon juice to the pan and pour the almonds and pan juices over the trout.

Serve immediately with plainly boiled potatoes and vegetables, or a salad.

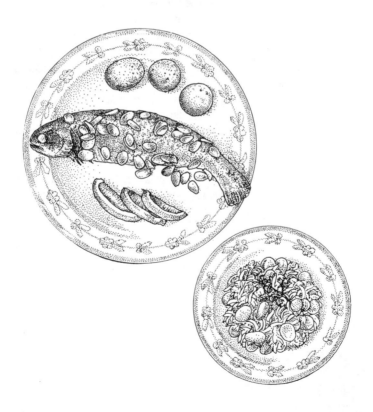

TROUT WITH BACON STUFFING

Serves 4

4 trout
40 g (1½ oz) butter
4 streaky bacon rashers, finely
  chopped
1 small onion, finely chopped
100 g (4 oz) mushrooms, finely
  chopped
50 g (2 oz) fresh brown breadcrumbs
2 tbsp fresh parsley, chopped
2 tsp lemon rind, grated
salt and pepper
1 egg

Heat the oven to 190°C (375°F) mark 5. Clean and gut the fish. Melt the butter and cook the bacon, onion and mushrooms over a low heat until soft and golden. Remove from the heat and mix with the breadcrumbs, parsley, lemon rind, salt, pepper and egg. Stuff the fish and secure with cocktail sticks. Arrange in a well-buttered oven-proof dish in a single layer. Bake for 25 minutes.

Serve with boiled or sauté potatoes and a vegetable.

HERBED TROUT IN CREAM SAUCE

Serves 4

4 trout
50 g (2 oz) butter
50 g (2 oz) dry breadcrumbs
1 small onion, finely chopped
2 tsp fresh sage, finely chopped
salt and pepper
225 g (8 oz) button mushrooms
150 ml (¼ pint) single cream

Heat the oven to 180°C (350°F) mark 4. Gut the trout, removing heads, although this is not necessary. Place in a buttered oven-proof dish and cover with buttered greaseproof paper. Bake for 20 minutes. Melt the butter and stir in the breadcrumbs, onion and sage. Cook over a low heat, stirring well, until the breadcrumbs are lightly golden. Season well with salt and pepper.

Slice the mushrooms and put into a pan with the cream. Cover and simmer for 3 minutes. Pour over the cooked trout and sprinkle the breadcrumb mixture on top. Continue baking for 5 minutes.

Serve hot with potatoes and a vegetable.

CRISP BROWN TROUT

Serves 4–6

6 brown trout
2 medium onions, chopped
1 tbsp oil
1 garlic clove, crushed
salt and pepper
25 g (1 oz) fresh white or brown
    breadcrumbs
50 g (2 oz) butter, melted
2 streaky bacon rashers
1 tbsp fresh parsley, chopped

Heat the oven to 180°C (350°F) mark 4. Clean and fillet the fish. Fry the onions gently in the oil until soft and golden. Stir in the garlic and season well. Place the trout in an oiled oven-proof dish. Cover with the onion mixture. Mix the breadcrumbs with butter and season with salt and pepper. Sprinkle on top of the onions. Bake for 25 minutes. While the fish are cooking, grill the bacon crisply and crumble into small pieces. Sprinkle the bacon and parsley on the fish and serve with boiled potatoes.

SUMMER PLAICE WITH COURGETTES

Serves 4

450 g (1 lb) courgettes
50 g (2 oz) butter
1 tbsp fresh parsley, chopped
1 tsp rosemary
salt and pepper
8 plaice fillets
25 g (1 oz) fresh breadcrumbs
25 g (1 oz) butter, melted
1 tbsp Parmesan cheese, grated

Heat the oven to 190°C (375°F) mark 5. Wipe the courgettes and slice them thinly without peeling. Melt the butter and fry the courgettes with the parsley and rosemary for 3 minutes. Remove from the heat, season well and place in the bottom of a shallow oven-proof dish. Fold the plaice fillets in half, skin side inwards and arrange on top of the courgettes. Sprinkle with breadcrumbs, drizzle with butter and sprinkle with Parmesan cheese. Bake for 20 minutes.

Serve at once with new potatoes and a salad.

PLAICE IN LEMON BUTTER

Serves 4

8 small plaice fillets
25 g (1 oz) plain flour
salt and pepper
75 g (3 oz) butter
1 tbsp oil
1 tbsp lemon juice
1 tbsp fresh parsley, chopped
lemon wedges to garnish

Dry the fish on kitchen paper. Season the flour with salt and pepper and coat the fish lightly on both sides. Put 50 g (2 oz) of the butter into a frying pan with the oil, and heat until the butter has melted. Fry the fish for 4 minutes on each side until cooked through and golden. Lift on to a warm serving dish.

Add the remaining butter, lemon juice and parsley to the pan and heat until golden brown. Pour over the fish, garnish with lemon wedges and serve at once.

BURNHAM PLAICE

Serves 2

2 small whole plaice
25 g (1 oz) brown breadcrumbs
1 celery stick, finely chopped
4 tbsp tomato juice
3 tbsp lemon juice
100 g (4 oz) peeled prawns

Garnish
 parsley sprigs
lemon wedges

Heat the oven to 200°C (400°F) mark 6. Clean and trim the fish but leave them whole. Place the fish on a flat surface with the white skin uppermost. Use a sharp knife to make a long slit down the backbone, and with the point of the knife, ease the flesh away from the backbone along both sides to make a pocket.

Mix the breadcrumbs with the celery, tomato juice, lemon juice and half the prawns. Pack the mixture into the pockets in the fish, allowing it to spill loosely. Place the fish in a shallow oven-proof dish. Cover with greased greaseproof paper and bake for 20 minutes. Lift the fish on to individual plates and garnish with remaining prawns, parsley and lemon wedges.

PLAICE ROLLS IN LEMON SAUCE

Serves 4

8 plaice fillets
100 g (4 oz) shrimps or prawns
15 g (½ oz) butter
15 g (½ oz) plain flour
275 ml (½ pint) milk
juice of 1 lemon
salt and pepper

Heat the oven to 180°C (350°F) mark 4.
Place the fish on a flat surface and divide the
shrimps or prawns between the fillets. Roll
the plaice round them and stand the fish
upright and close together in a greased
oven-proof dish. Melt the butter and work
in the flour. Stir in the milk over a low heat
and cook gently until the sauce thickens.
Remove from the heat and stir in the lemon
juice. Season well and pour over the fish.
Bake for 25 minutes.
 Serve with potatoes and vegetables.

HAKE BAKE

Serves 4

50 g (2 oz) butter
1 garlic clove, crushed
2 medium onions, sliced
175 g (6 oz) mushrooms, sliced
1 tsp fresh mixed herbs
4 hake cutlets or steaks (or cod)
salt and pepper
25 g (1 oz) fresh brown or white
 breadcrumbs

Heat the oven to 190°C (375°F) mark 5.
Melt the butter and reserve half of it. Use
the rest to cook the garlic, onions,
mushrooms and herbs over a low heat for
5 minutes, stirring well. Place in an oven-
proof dish. Season the fish on both sides
with salt and pepper and place it on top of
the vegetables. Sprinkle with breadcrumbs
and the remaining butter. Bake for
30 minutes.